ART START ANIMALS

How to Draw with Simple Shapes

Barbara Soloff Levy

DOVER PUBLICATIONS, INC.

Mineola, New York

Note

Drawing is fun, and it's easy, too! Using simple shapes and lines, you'll learn how to draw a cute cat, a happy hippopotamus, and many other favorite animals. Here's how: The steps for drawing each animal are shown on two facing pages. First, look at the top of the pages. Here are the shapes and lines that you will use for your picture. Just draw what you see in Step 1 in the space below. Then add the shape or shapes for Steps 2, 3, and 4. To make it even easier, each time a new shape is added, it is shown in color. It's a good idea to use a pencil with an eraser, just in case you decide to change part of your drawing.

When you're done, color in your pictures any way you wish, using crayons, markers, or colored pencils. After you have finished all of your drawings, you can think of more animals to draw. Let's get started!

Bibliographical Note

ART START ANIMALS: How to Draw with Simple Shapes is a new work, first published by Dover Publications, Inc., in 2010.

International Standard Book Number
ISBN-13: 978-0-486-47677-3
ISBN-10: 0-486-47677-4

Manufactured in the United States by Courier Corporation
47677405   2014
www.doverpublications.com

ART START
ANIMALS

How to Draw with Simple Shapes

USE THESE SHAPES AND LINES TO DRAW YOUR PICTURE

1.

2.

3.

4.

USE THESE SHAPES AND LINES TO DRAW YOUR PICTURE

1.

2.

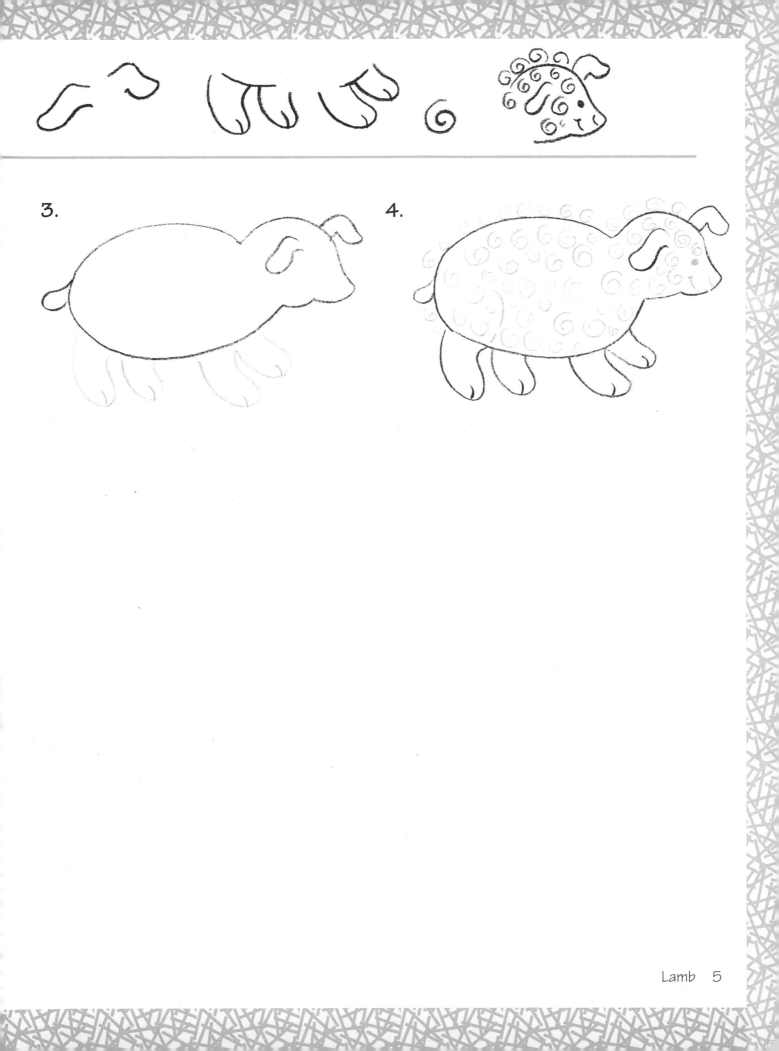

3.

4.

USE THESE SHAPES AND LINES TO DRAW YOUR PICTURE

1.

2.

3.

4.

USE THESE SHAPES AND LINES TO DRAW YOUR PICTURE

1.

2.

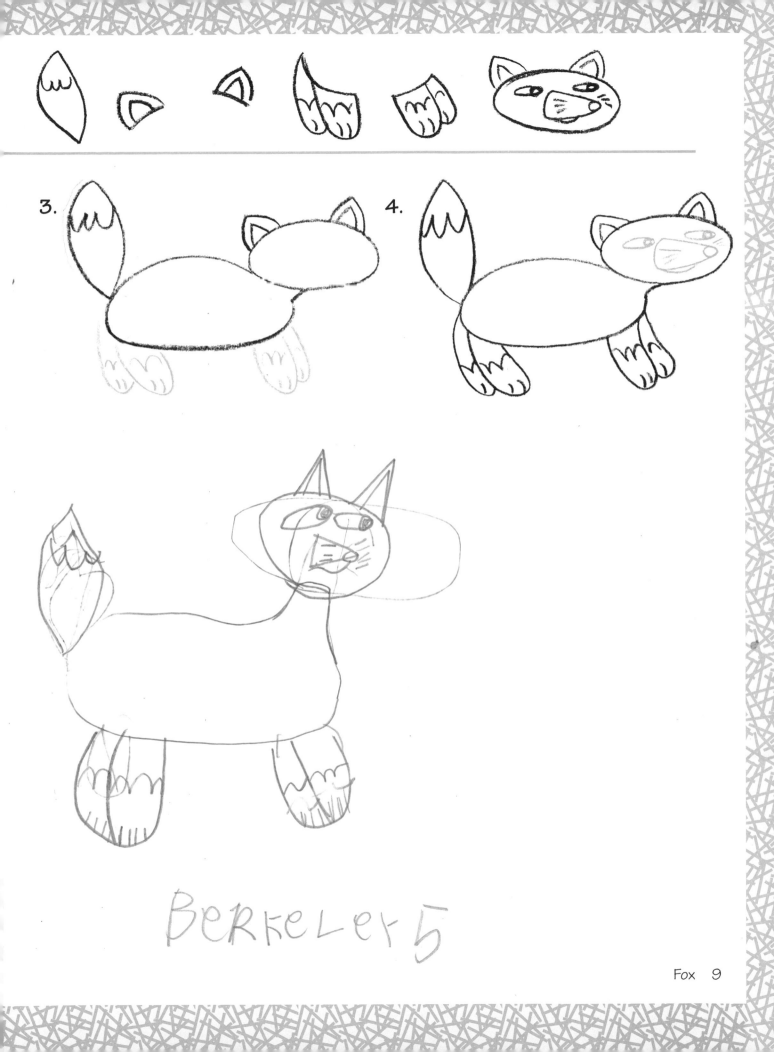

3.

4.

BERKELEY 5

USE THESE SHAPES AND LINES TO DRAW YOUR PICTURE

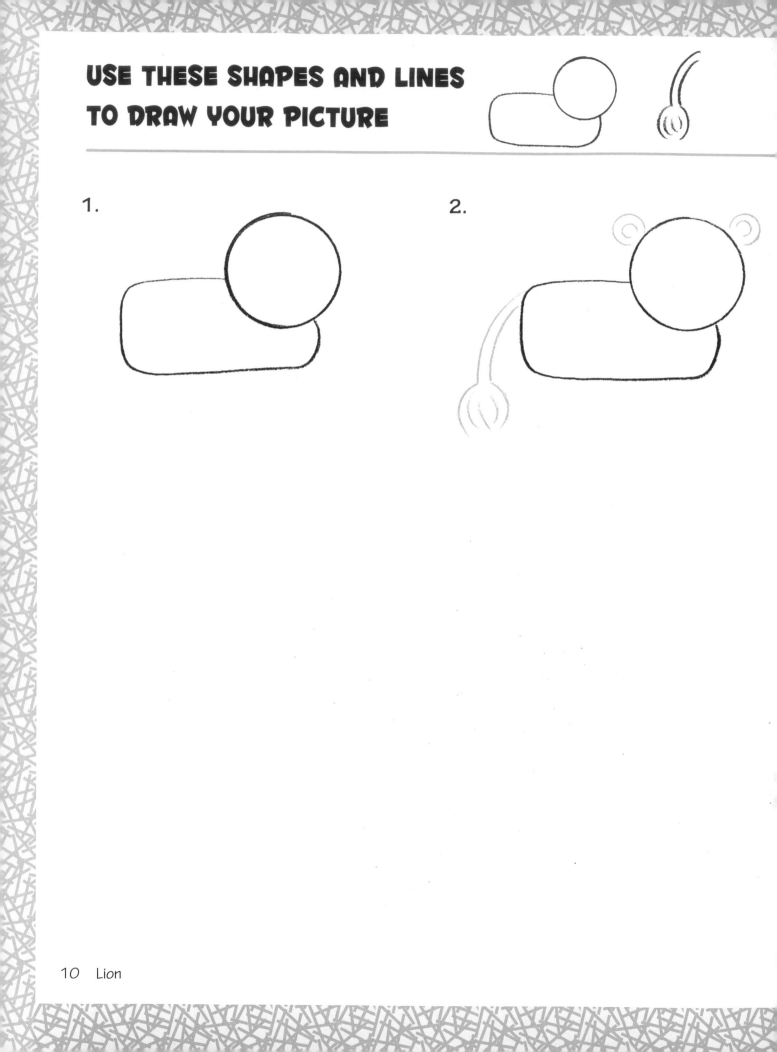

1.

2.

3.

4.

5

USE THESE SHAPES AND LINES TO DRAW YOUR PICTURE

1.

2.

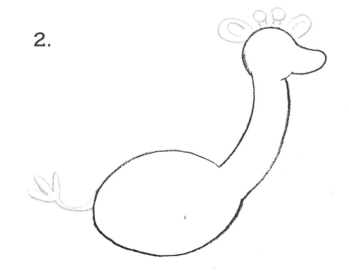

3.

4.

USE THESE SHAPES AND LINES TO DRAW YOUR PICTURE

1.

2.

3.

4.

USE THESE SHAPES AND LINES TO DRAW YOUR PICTURE

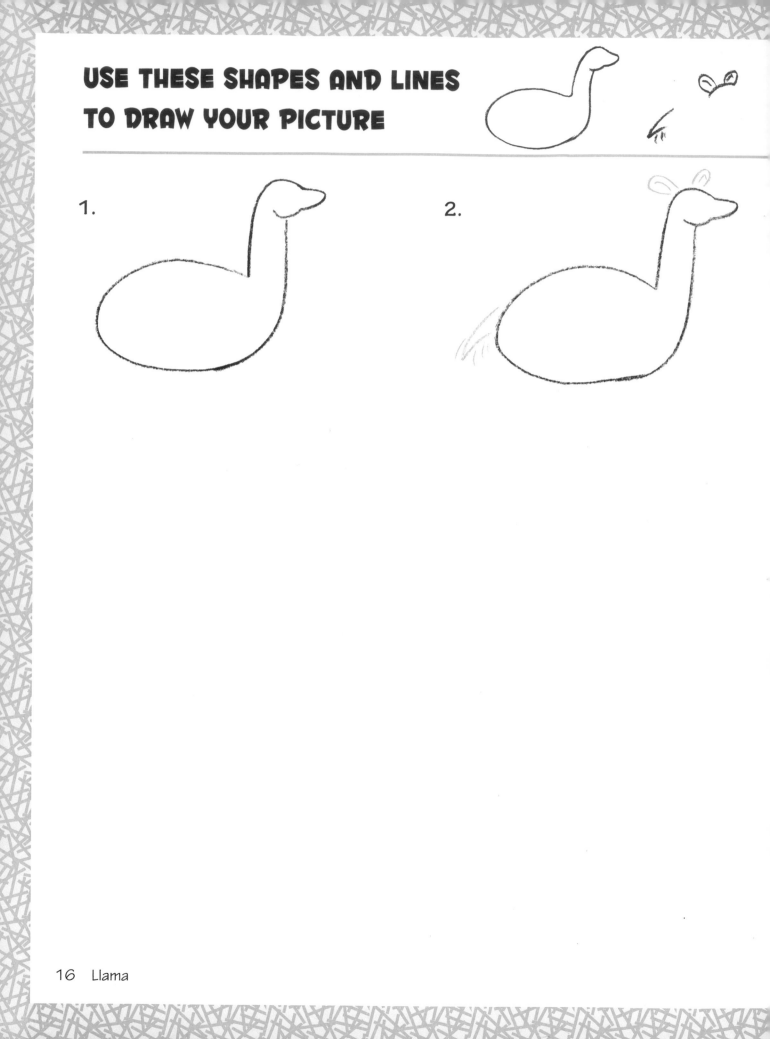

1.

2.

3.

4.

USE THESE SHAPES AND LINES TO DRAW YOUR PICTURE

1.

2.

3.

4.

USE THESE SHAPES AND LINES TO DRAW YOUR PICTURE

1.

2.

20   Dog

3.

4.

USE THESE SHAPES AND LINES TO DRAW YOUR PICTURE

1

2.

3.

4.

USE THESE SHAPES AND LINES TO DRAW YOUR PICTURE

1.

2.

3.

4.

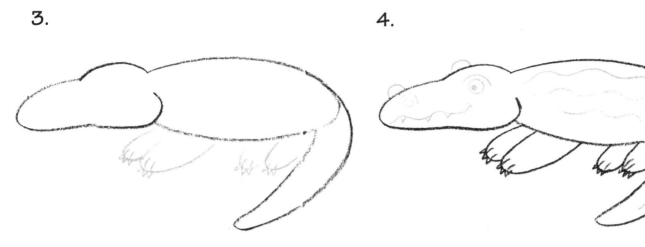

USE THESE SHAPES AND LINES TO DRAW YOUR PICTURE

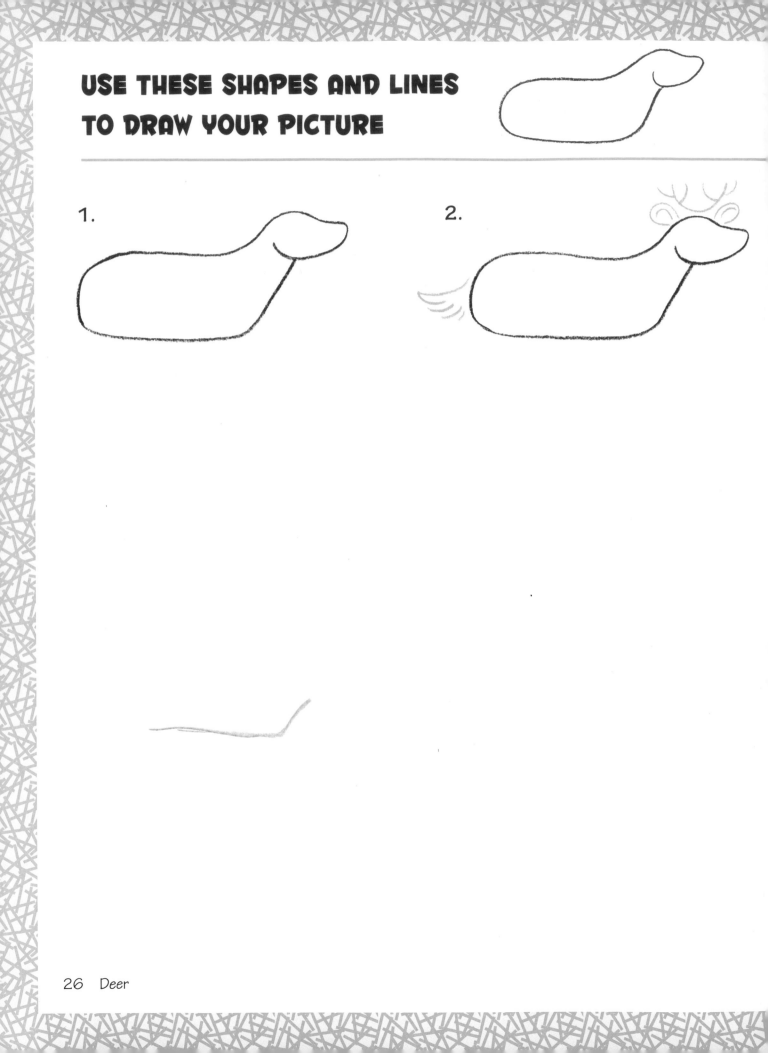

1.

2.

3.

4.

USE THESE SHAPES AND LINES
TO DRAW YOUR PICTURE

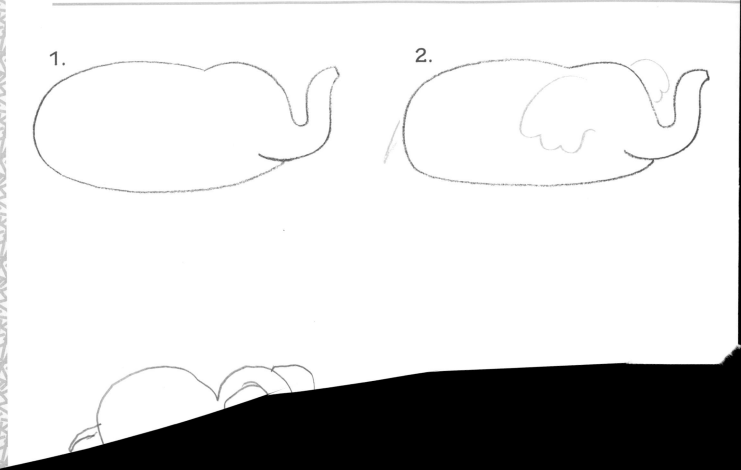

1.

2.

3.

4.

USE THESE SHAPES AND LINES TO DRAW YOUR PICTURE

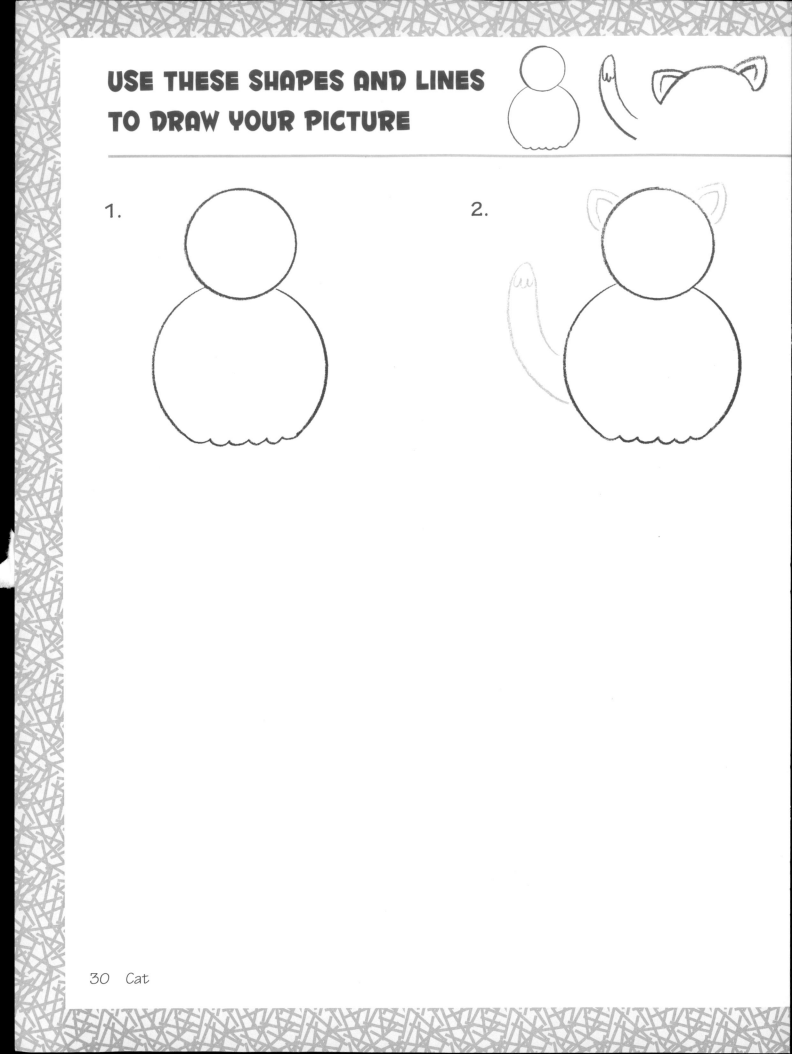

1.

2.

3.

4.

USE THESE SHAPES AND LINES TO DRAW YOUR PICTURE

1.

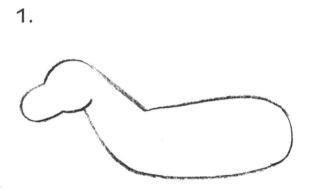

2.

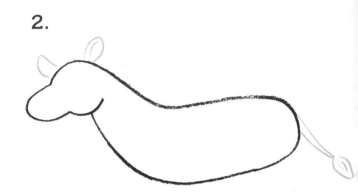

3.

4.

USE THESE SHAPES AND LINES TO DRAW YOUR PICTURE

1.

2.

4.

1.

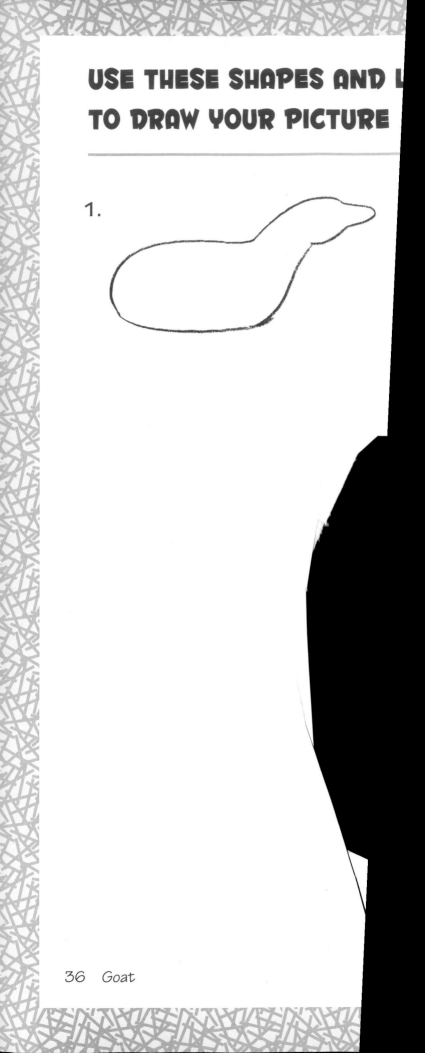

3.

4.

USE THESE SHAPES AND LINES TO DRAW YOUR PICTURE

1.

2.

3.

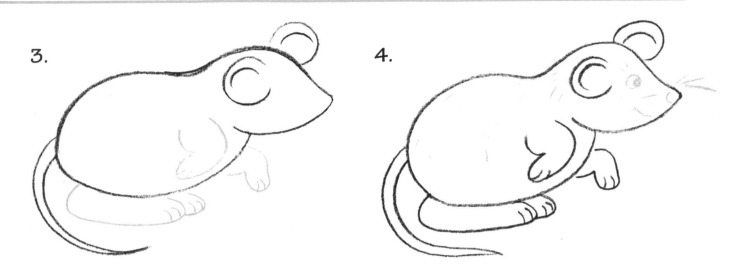

4.

USE THESE SHAPES AND LINES TO DRAW YOUR PICTURE

1.

2.

3.

4.

USE THESE SHAPES AND LINES TO DRAW YOUR PICTURE

1.

2.

3.

4.

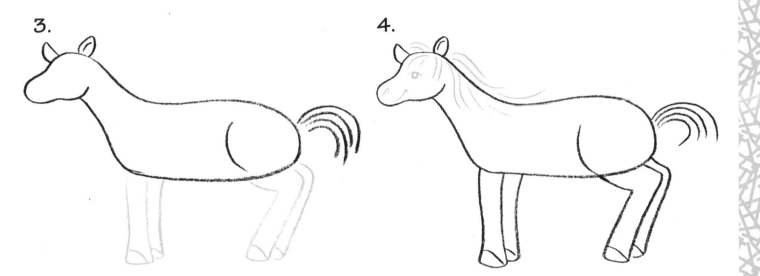

USE THESE SHAPES AND LINES TO DRAW YOUR PICTURE

1.

2.

3.

4.

USE THESE SHAPES AND LINES TO DRAW YOUR PICTURE

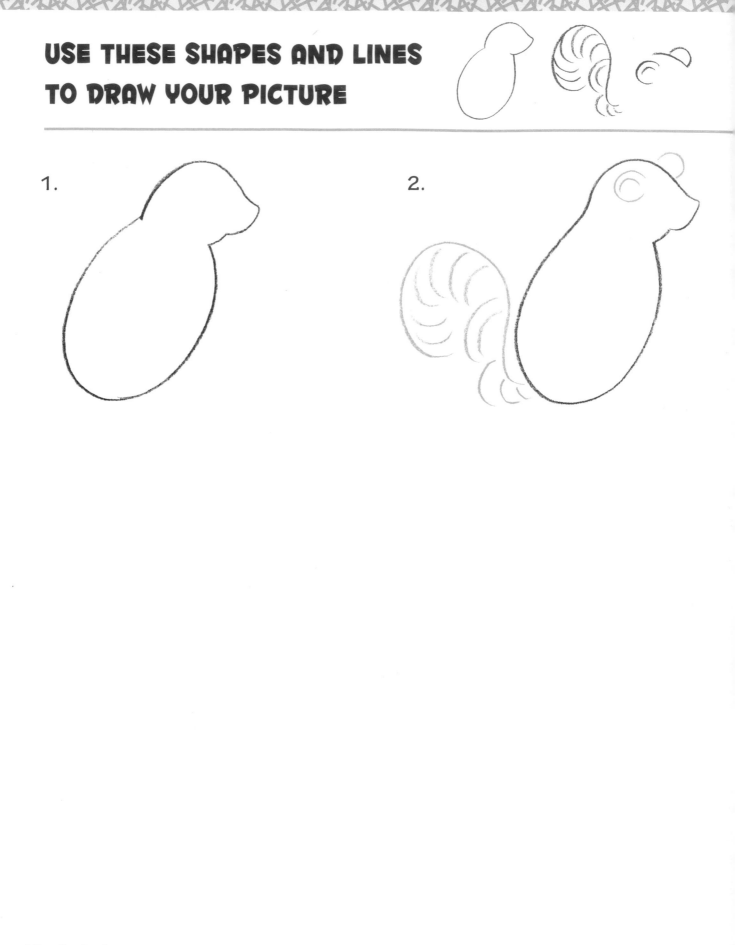

1.

2.

3.

4.

USE THESE SHAPES AND LINES TO DRAW YOUR PICTURE

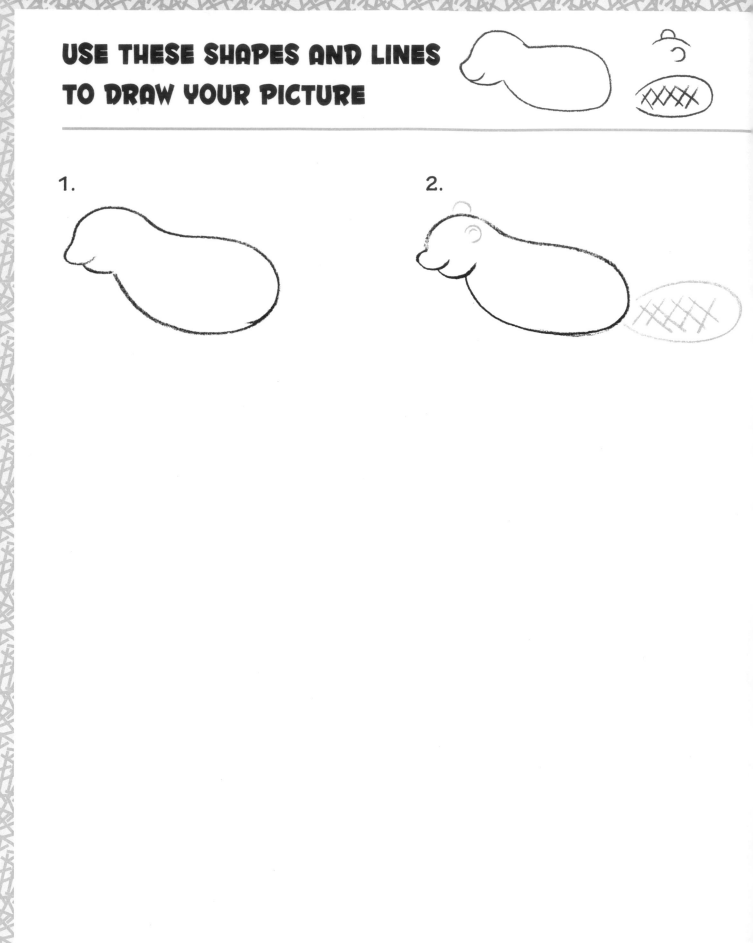

1.

2.

3.

4.

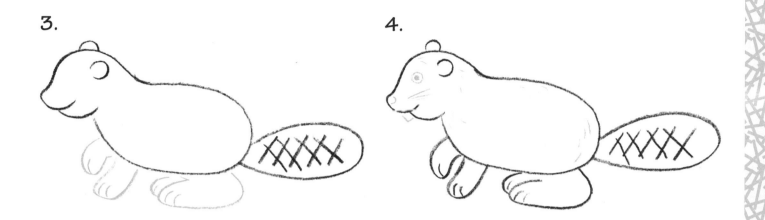

USE THESE SHAPES AND LINES TO DRAW YOUR PICTURE

1.

2.

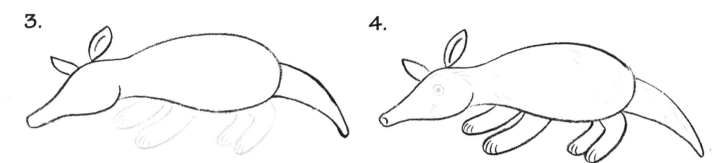

3.

4.

USE THESE SHAPES AND LINES TO DRAW YOUR PICTURE

1.

2.

3.

4.

USE THESE SHAPES AND LINES TO DRAW YOUR PICTURE

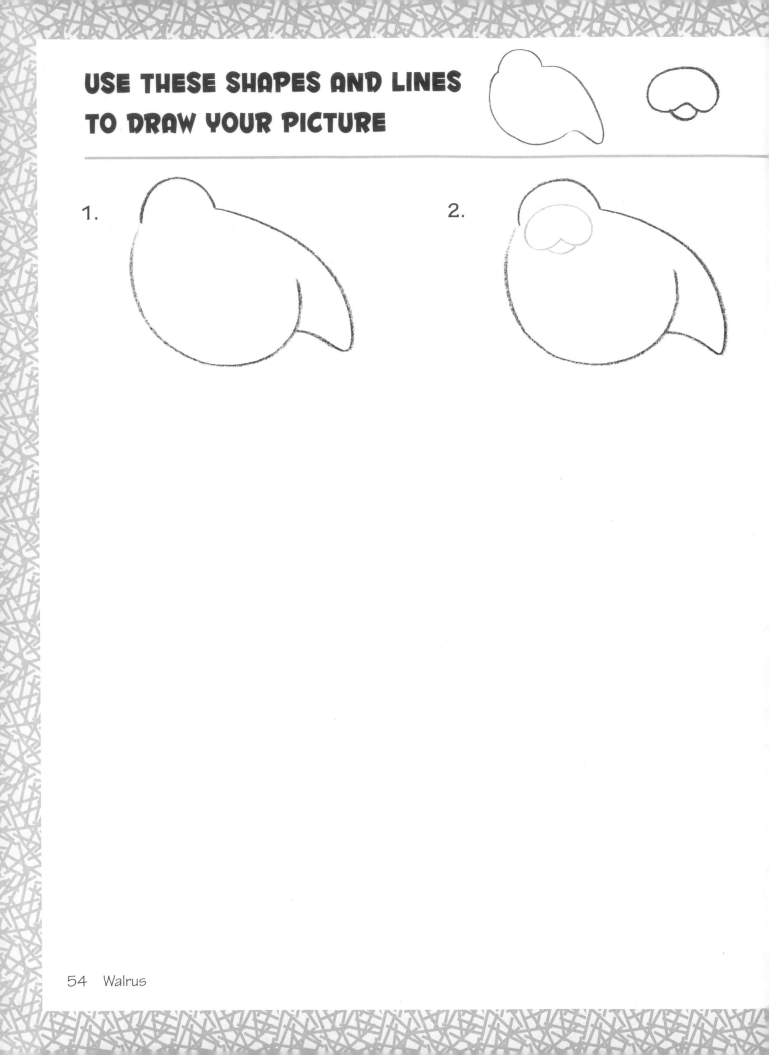

1.

2.

3.

4.

USE THESE SHAPES AND LINES TO DRAW YOUR PICTURE

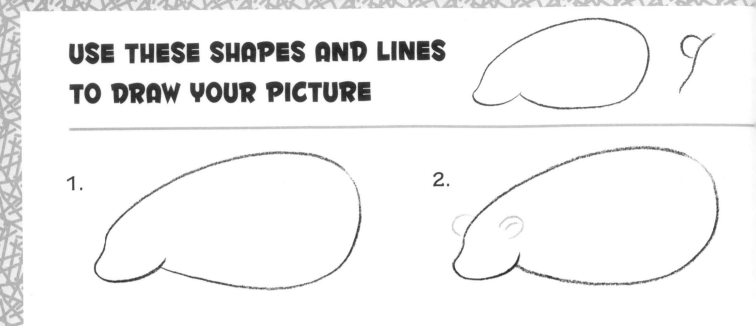

1.

2.

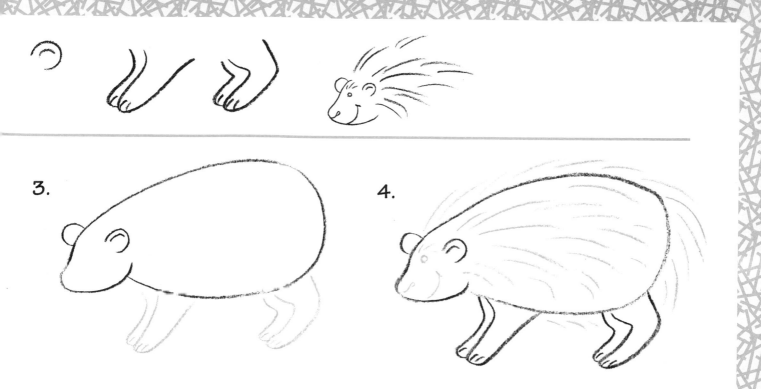

3.

4.

USE THESE SHAPES AND LINES TO DRAW YOUR PICTURE

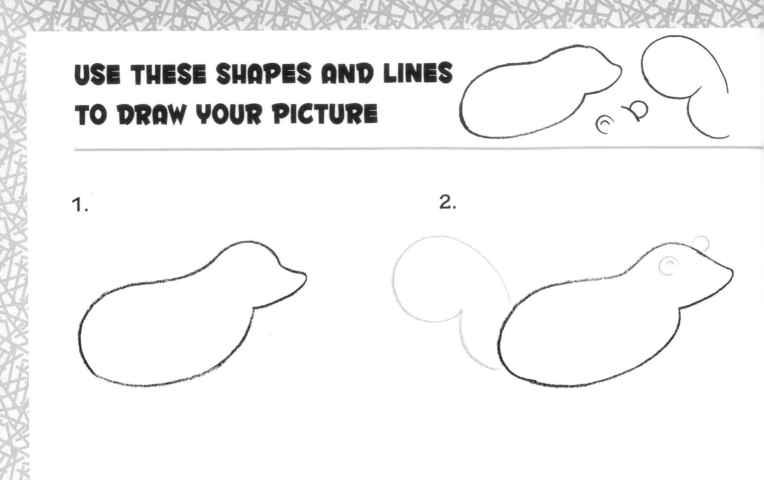

1.

2.

3.

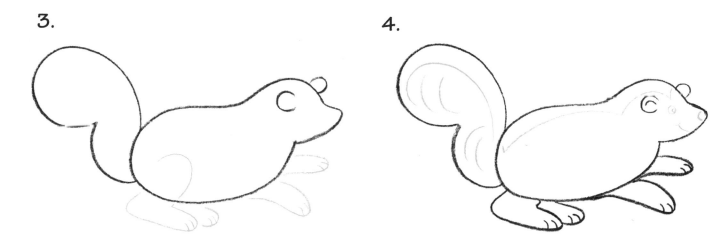

4.

USE THESE SHAPES AND LINES TO DRAW YOUR PICTURE

1.

2.

3.

4.